**ALSO BY PETER GIZZI**

*Archeophonics*
*In Defense of Nothing: Selected Poems, 1987–2011*
*Threshold Songs*
*The Outernationale*
*Some Values of Landscape and Weather*
*Artificial Heart*
*Periplum and other poems*

**NOW IT'S DARK**

# NOW IT'S DARK
# PETER GIZZI

WESLEYAN UNIVERSITY PRESS • MIDDLETOWN, CONNECTICUT

Wesleyan Poetry

Wesleyan University Press
Middletown CT 06459
www.wesleyan.edu/wespress

© 2020 Peter Gizzi
All rights reserved
Printed in Canada
Book design by Rick Myers Art Utility

Hardcover ISBN 978-0-8195-7986-7
Paperback ISBN 978-0-8195-7987-4
Ebook ISBN 978-0-8195-7988-1

Library of Congress Cataloging-in-Publication
Data appear at the back of the book.

5 4 3 2

## CONTENTS

**1. LYRIC** *1*

**2. GARLAND** *55*

**3. NOCTURNE** *87*

**4. CODA** *99*

*Acknowledgments 111*
*Index of Titles 113*

for my brother Tom

*also gone*

*I'll meet you where we survive.*

– Jason Molina

# 1. LYRIC

## SPEECH ACTS FOR A DYING WORLD

A field sparrow
is at my window,
tapping at its reflection,
a tired
antique god
trying to communicate

it's getting to me

as I set out to sing
the nimbus of flora
under a partly mottled sky

as I look at the end
and sing so what,
sing live now,
thinking why not

I'm listening and
receiving now
and it feeds me,
I'm always hungry

when the beautiful
is too much to carry
inside my winter

when my library is full of loss
full of wonder

as the polis is breaking
and casts a shadow
over all of me,
thinking of it

when the shadows fall
in ripples, when
the medium I work in
is deathless and

I'm living inside
one great example
of stubbornness

as my head is stove-in
by a glance, as the day's
silver-tipped buds sway in union,
waving to the corporate sky

when I said work
and meant lyric

when I thought I was done
with the poem as a vehicle
to understand violence

I thought I was done
with the high-toned
shitty world

done with the voice and
its constituent pap

call down the inherited
phenomenal world
when it's raining in the book,
lost to the world
in an abundance of world

like listening to a violin
when the figure isn't native
but the emotion is

when everything is snow
and what lies ahead
is a mesmer's twirling locket

I thought I was done
with the marvel
of ephemeral shadow play,
the great design and all that

I thought I was done
with time, its theatricality,
glamour, and guff

gusting cloud, I see you,
I become you
in my solitary thinging,
here in partial light

when I said voice,
I meant the whole unholy grain of it,
it felt like paradise

meaning rises and sets,
now a hunter overhead
now a bear at the pole
and the sound of names

the parade of names

## THAT I SAW THE LIGHT ON NONOTUCK AVENUE

That every musical note is a flame, native in its own tongue.

That between bread and ash, there is fire.

That the day swells and crests.

That I found myself born into it with sirens and trucks going by out here in a poem.

That there are other things that go into poems like the pigeon, cobalt, dirty windows, sun.

That I have seen skin in marble, eye in stone.

That the information I carry is mostly bacterial.

That I am a host.

That the ghost of the text is unknown.

That I live near an Air Force base and the sound in the sky is death.

That sound like old poetry can kill us.

That there are small things in the poem: paper clips, gauze, tater tots, knives.

That there can also be emptiness fanning out into breakfast rolls, macadam, stars.

That I am hungry.

That I seek knowledge of the ancient sycamore that also lives in the valley where I live.

That I call to it.

That there are airships overhead.

That I live alone in my head out here in a poem near a magical tree.

That I saw the light on Nonotuck Avenue and heard the cry of a dove recede into a rustle.

That its cry was quiet light falling into a coffin.

That it altered me.

That today the river is a camera obscura, bending trees.

That I sing this of metallic shimmer, sing the sky, the song, all of it and wonder if I am dying would you come back for me?

## EVERY DAY I WANT TO FLY MY KITE

Give the world
to the world,
time to the flood,
give ash to gardens
and grain to trees.
I am not cowed
by the superlative
nature in trees.
I am lifted
and see petals opening.

Give the freckled ground
to sun,
give sepulcher
to sky,
to song.
I am not one
to disregard thrush,
diminish sparrow.

Give the arrow
to lovers,
night to lavender,
lavender to sleep,
to wing
to want
to wound
to wonder
the night's watch,
the optical dawn.

Give water to stone,
stone to echo.
In the mosaic
the dove's wings
are made of bits
and stone.
The world is like this.

If I saw it
I felt it.
If I felt it
I learned from it.

And when the moon
opens the horizon,
that's Tuesday gone.

The moon
the silk
the corn
the rail.
I felt this and
it stuck to me
one midnight.
I was mewling.

I was alive with fancy
and silk and stuff.
I was stuffing for a chair,
a doll.
I was blinking
and crying and.

Now the word
falling.
Now other rains.

Now organics
cyclones and seeds.
The deadly swoon
in strength and
with color
and the sound
of crows and
their platinum sheen
feeding the sky.
Flames and greatness
towing the names.

Give home
to the horizon,
horizon to mystery,
mercy, meaning.
I thought I
might try to
head out
the door.
The door.
It doesn't
matter.

I go as long
as I go and if
you're there
to sparrow.
Sparrow.

# THE PRESENT IS CONSTANT ELEGY

Those years when I was alive, I lived the era of the fast car.

There were silhouettes in gold and royal blue, a half-light in tire marks across a field—Times when the hollyhocks spoke.

There were weeds in a hopescape as in a painted backdrop there is also a face.

And then I found myself when the poem wanted me in pain writing this.

The sky was always there but useless—And what of the blue phlox, onstage and morphing.

Chance blossoms so quickly, it's a wonder we recognize anything, wanting one love to walk out of the ground.

Passion comes from a difficult world—I'm sick of twilight, when the light is crushed, time unravels its string.

Along the way I discovered a voice, a sun-stroked path choked with old light, a ray already blown.

Look at the world, its veil.

## NOW IT'S DARK

Not the easiest day I'm having, clouds banking
   and I dropped my signal.
I was trying to find my shoes and thought
I am overpowered by the gigantism
   of commercial governing.
As I looked for my shoes this morning
the thought was where am I going?
There isn't a place I can walk out from
   under this chemical sky.
So I thought I would write a poem.
I thought I would try and make art.
But the chemicals seep into everything.
Reader, if I could I would bring back for you
   a sun made in crayon.
A sun unformed in the paper sky.
I wonder the paper that made me.
Being human I know that paper makes my mind.
Strange pulp reminding me I am far away.

When my brother could no longer speak
   I said Tommy I got this
even if I don't want this, I'll sing for you.
When my brother had no voice there was only the couch
   and a wooden floor
the ceiling and the TV with nothing blaring.
When my brother lost his voice I lost my childhood
lost the sun over sand in some place I can't remember
   in Rhode Island summer.
So far from myself in a body I can't remember.
To no longer remember my body as a child.
To no longer remember today all that was.
Van Gogh was tormented by the sun and why not.
A constant blade-searing light that kills and cures.
I am not comforted by the cold stability
   of universal laws
though one day I'll die and think, that's ok.
At least I'm writing and it makes a party in the dark.
A zombie feature that connects me to the undying.
I read every moment is an opportunity for grace
and think every moment is a possibility of art.

I tie my shoes and now I am standing alone
   in some inky light.
Yesterday I passed a Budget Motel next to
   the Peoples Bank.
If there's some connection it's lost on me.
My heart lost on me.
Weather like thought dissolves into static,
a wiggy keepsake like nesting dolls of my
   spiritual blank.
Sky opening into blank.
I thought grief is a form of grace.
Then someone said the thing about money
   is that it's money.
I live on the edge of an expanding circumference
   alone in some inky light.
Now rain turns the world to constant applause.
The day is uncoupled.
All there is is thunder as the house decays
   into a sound like me.
Freezing rain with silver seems to be speaking
   and isn't asking me anything.
Just doing its thing in the gray morning.

I was down with materialism but
   wanted mystery.
I've asked myself a lot of questions like
   why the days cascade
swiping left for life, right for lost.
All of it a dumb show.
All of me invested in poetry and the
   arrogance of this.
Wanting to transpose loneliness.
Why not take on the next life
   with its silence.
On my desk there are small plastic creatures.
The light on them is unrealistic.
It uncouples me.
Or the sight of serious windows opening out
   onto serious lawns.
This must be a government building.
This must be the anodyne room of
   a hospital beeping.
Every pronouncement on the feed, alien.
I'm in this corridor wandering a mind.
But the day is past caring.

The rhythmus is blooming at the beginning
   of the way back when.
I am sick with tradition and its weak signaling.
Sparkling eclogues drift and contribute
   little to the cause.
I am an incident trapped in thick description.
Just google it.
Dust jacket shows some rubbing,
   near fine in cloth.

# THE AFTERLIFE OF PAPER

the last best love is language in the mouth

the last best hope for joy doesn't forget

a besting sensation

the last stranger blooming on the tongue

a compass rose blooming internally

laying down track

riding the rails

wake unto me

## OUT OF THE WORLD IN REAL TIME

The silence in this room is causing a looping effect.

All I see is wood grain and air when it's raining in the true north of the poem.

It gives purchase to the page. It gives courage.

I want to tell you this isn't just all song.

I want to say this scrap of paper has sky in it.

To be lost in its yesterglow casting shadows upon a silent h.

H for hour and honor, honest and heir, also ghost, ghastly, ghetto, etc.

Who knew such light could come from torn paper.

What comes first, flag or paper? Voting or votive?

There are distances. The whole archival light blooming.

I recast words to say everything touched by light remembers that light.

To recast light that touched marble strewn from time, lying among weeds and trash—

worn from human traffic and ordinary songs.

In my head, a flywheel unable to power anything other than song and all that's left is survival—

some old piece of canvas flapping in the gale.

The oak creaks and the air is keening.

That green light could only be oxygen.

I am witness, a copy of rain in June, a glinting vowel.

## LAST POEM

The dove and the grass share
a genetic relationship.
These things that fit.
I fit with the night sky
where candles manufacture
classic scenes.
There is a constant
banging in my head.
Not sure what it looks like.
I wanted more.
The green light rushing in.
But the light is strobe-like
against the pane.
I am lost inside it
and have been traveling a long time.
My compass spinning.
So I let go of the world
and the world came back.

The sun leaves us homesick.
It is the mundo of existence.
Hangman, wait,
I am sick with sunset
as I wait for the past
to recuperate
lines into a presence.
I awake to a wanting
other than time.
To see past oneself
over here in a poem.
Sound winging.

The world will burst
into green and fall to dirt.
The dirt will green
when the colors come back
into the words
and these colors speak
not for me but for you.
Thinking of all the people
thinking of people
they won't see again.

And so it goes, high noon
where I worry labor
and its discontents.

I hate hubble photos of the sun,
it looks so fucked up.
I mean, look out man,
the world isn't stable.
A dog whimpers
in the house next door.
These elements nature.
The orders of spring,
for instance, confuse
the speech mechanism.
The lodestone came singing
but the breakage
in the signal was permanent.

Middle of the night
electrons hurt most.
This is a metaphor.
Though I hurt and wonder

unhinged by maybe

and wave to the unconscious.

Punctuation like damage.

Damage like applause.

The hum of the fridge

is all there is.

Some days, truth is.

I don't got a clue.

I was in the midst of death

when I wrote the poem of life.

I didn't know.

## NOW IT'S DARK

No one gave me a greater thing
than their time.
But the old song,
worn from use,
is with me again.
So much of it
behind me now.
In front of me a slow season,
when a face passes
into a name.
Last night the moon was lolling
9 degrees over the horizon
but I didn't know.
I was in a fever dream
downloading ravens into my skull.
An unkindness of them.
This is called what it's like
to sleep alone for years.

It means all these years to remain
untouched wrote the poem.
I use my mouth to say goodbye,
fever dream, raven, skull.
To say like a flower, little dust.
To say what of it.
The world is close today
and elegy is my tonic.
I recast language in hope
of recovering the red oak
my neighbors felled.
It lived over a hundred years, glowing.
Now, neither music or rhyme,
just night, tin, and sky.

## SKY BURIAL

The robin that lives in my yard
also lives in me. This is the interior,
while the state unwinds across
a vast expanse splitting the sky.
It is all of it and more;
these things were passages
of the light-born afternoon
cascading then expanding
like a flange around the day.
Yes, the day, staccato
in its azure and gold banner;
then one learns, as one learns
from twilight, how to look
through here, and not here, grinning.
The wisteria out my window
is waving, up, down, up,
it's so far away though, outside.
I'm in here where the word is opening.

There are distances, the whole
tonal range blooming,
clarity of attenuated looking,
a payload delivering meaningful dust.
It's a good day to die.

## INSIDE OUT LOUD

And then
the day
became fact.
Burned
beyond
description.
Though
why waste
a day
with description.
Better to
say why
waste
the poem
with trumpets.
Better to
say lilac,
to say war,
the room
I live in.

The collapse
of interiority
happened
in my time.
In my time
I was a
bewildered
subject,
a ghost
hungry for
selfhood.
I was walking
and talking.
I thought of you.
I think of you,
ghost.
It's impossible
to see
the flight
against
the void
I come from

inside

the extremes

where I

really lived.

The other me

hidden

and darker.

I kept

my language

closer.

These

redacted

documents

inside.

Writing

is one thing.

Pain is

the same thing.

I am

a stranger

in this.

I use

the words

haunted
and life
because
you can
see them.
But it's more
like spinning
light in
a dark room.
A catastrophic
light.
I have seen it
before but
if there's
a way
forward
I've yet
to find it.
I will sigh
at winter's
psychodrama
of wind.

There is
a greensward
inside.
A reclamation
in small things.
There is
a hill and
on this hill
I see
another hill.
The bridges
were a
natural iron.
Ferns bowed
in the gale.
Leaves
came to
ground.
What wind
brought me,
wanting
to see

the truth
in green.
Sequestered
here,
there is
a purpose.
There is
a density
to sight.
To see is
an organic
thing.
Sunday was
like this,
an unwavering
lively
occurring,
stupefied
and restless.

# LETTER TO THE GHOST WORLD

The night-air in freshets speaks its volumetrics in the park, enchantments parade across asphalt into cobalt light. Nothing more real than a power line overhead in midsummer, late night breeze rushing the bushes and limbs. Is life the tree whose crown is splayed, pruned, and misshapen to allow the line to blast through undisturbed, or is life the intruder, somnolent, steady, and the world around it, the branches, changed by its presence? An anonymous cord moving through the day and lying awake at night thinking what and what if. The head sways with wind, the line gives a bit. Even if fixed in place the air is air.

## VASTATION

What about the polar lights
that touch earth.
I have seen them on my voyage.
Vivid is my ship.
Looking there
I found an iridescence
opening a chatter
between self and ether.
I found a shoreline.
I found a face.
An uncharted face.
What can be said of love.
That I saw a ray breaking through,
saw the night pouring down.
The sky speaks to me and says
you will find shards,
unattended joy, pieces of sorrow.
Will sail past hell to get here.
Like a match struck,

there is the flare
and the midnight around it.
When the world comes back
you'll see a mound of earth
more dazzling than all the sea.
A blossom cutting cool air.
It's all there in the cello
and the bow, the tree
and its croaking.
It's all there in the soft tissue.
A musical flood.
The sky speaks to me
and says, I survived.
Says, there is this day
that can happen
when a face opens.
Now, that's all I see.
I was happy to die
if it meant I could live.

# THE INGENUITY OF ANIMAL SURVIVAL

Deep in the enzyme is the shape of home.

Deep in the code is the architecture to nest.

The Robin collects mud with its beak along with twigs and pieces of down and feathers too.

The Grouse burrows into a subnivean world for heat and shelter.

The Raven uses branches and breaks them off with its weight and its beak, it papers its nest with bits of fur and debris.

The Goose sheds her chest feathers to line the chamber.

Sorrow is long.

When will I return to my country?

## THE FACE IS A POLITICAL ANIMAL

The face is a political animal,
an antique washboard,
pitted sign, a blooming nightshade
just out the window

the face is an heirloom rose,
rainbow, cloud show
and intermittent shower

the face is lettered,
a *minzah*, garden,
*espace vert*, *giardino*,
arbor, and bier

face of granite
and years, emotive
sun inside sun,
inside fire, a signal flare

the face is a voting booth,
ballot, bumper sticker
and prayer, a Sunday
walk about a lake

is a crow's nest,
a noose, a long
distance call

a down-home rodeo,
a homemade kazoo
is homespun,
homegrown

a parade float

a worn bunting
distorting
through the pane.

## SUNDAY'S EMPIRE

The roofs speak
as light over
the scaped silence.

A cacophony
of shapes
kicks off into sky.

People live here
in the quiet
a day undresses.

Tones shaking out.

## ARCHIVAL LIGHT

I love how
light comes
through
charcoal
on a page,
a particular
paper light
that archivists
and lovers
of books
also live in
or it lives
within us.
But you left
me on the daze
of sun left
on the table,
a warm
wood light

that was pleasant

as the goneness

set up inside me.

The goneness

that is me.

What of

the days

we walked

to green.

What did

it mean

when you said

I am closer

to you now

as you disappeared

into blue

unfolding

into blue.

I get

confused.

I live in

goodbye.

I live in
late light
going darker.
Late light
on a page,
on skin,
in my life.

## SOME JOY FOR MORNING

Now the connection with spring has dissolved.

Now that hysteria is blooming.

Says every day I want to fly my kite.

Says what's a grammar when you is no longer you.

My world is hydrogen burning in space and in the fullness of etc.

I have read the news and learned nothing.

I try to understand the whooshing overhead.

But for a little light now.

I didn't realize the tree was weeping.

How was I to know I am not alone.

Wild light.

# SUNSHINE

Of what. Was wing.
Was bright all afternoon.

Was nothing
more than
collapsing into
the crisp March
late-winter air.

This sheaf of light.
It doesn't help.

Nowhere to tune
my voice, waiting.
My mental furniture
breaking.

I have blood
in my veins

and we go on
together trying
to decode
the swath of evil
across our sun-
sovereign bodies.

All I want
is the word
to reveal the day.

Want to understand
the this in that,
want this, got that
and ran with it.

Also the stanzas
against the capital
reeling from might.

Got to be with
the peoples who

said no, and
then said yes.

The art of
the collective
as it collapses
into a poem.

Sometimes there
is a poem
and says my life.

Says what. Says wing.

## THE BLOSSOM IS STRONGER THAN US

but to want the beauty of the hollyhock

Augustine sad, reading in the alcove

so much sand and wind with us all this time

so many bullets and boys crying mother before the weather

but why after all this nothing but the changing weather

playing the changes, the children

in the magnitude, love

in the horror, love

# 2. GARLAND

## MARIGOLD & CABLE

*i.*

In morning's coloratura
a magick eye plays tricks
under the ongoing mossy
cloud-mass, exhilarating
triangles and timpani softly
in silt air, in the blanketed
nowhere of now

O silk, O air,
speak softly
in the blankety
almost now,
to be triaged
in the whorl,
see it, tranquil,
joyful, merging
from the dark
beginning to full,
chant largo

It's beginning to whorl,
chant largo, how
lovely the blooming
aurora, chapel hymns,
and hush we cry
accepting death, coo,
in the dark, lovely

Deathward we coo,
darkly we love
in the ex, the far sun
carpeting, the clouds
stilling, the senses
of serpent inside
the ongoing aberration
in the eye, scaled, glassy

These indiscretions
in the eye, scaled,
saucy, the sun
over aphasia, we
didn't ask for this
wintering rust
but elegy is tonic
on the stoop,
far candle

Rust and elegy
on the stoop,
the far candle
gutters, o clock
your music
is unwritten,
even if
on heavy days,
the bright
systems sing,
smeared gold

These sonic

systems

smeared golden,

a blank wall

opening,

and forward

the hen-cock,

bright comedy

of grain, incipience

cried the dove,

and all of

the skeleton

The dove cries

alpha through

her scales, throws

an indignant vowel,

one might find

hair falling, pitiless

verse, a mind

at rest, flawed

in falling dust

Breathlessness
and awe at rest
in falling dust,
pshaw, that mass
of freak-sun
greater than
old rebellion,
cold poetry
in the heart,
rude, undone,
the grass is full

Poetry's sun,
freaked, full, un-
governed, ruddy,
the morphic
clouds impress,
the head blooming,
in this man
paperwhites,
black lines glare,
Euclid sings
in the heart

*ii.*

Euclid sings to the arc,
black lines blooming,
Saturn, the sudden
evening, nothing to do
with stars, it had no aversion
to the quill-like air
in this whirring vista

In the star-like whir,

perpetually quilled,

the drums and trumpets

push back thunder,

to meditate on a small owl

above, just hovering

To meditate
the small owl
hovering
above justice,
sing this,
at home
in clairvoyance,
moonlight
crumbles into
thinglessness
trilling, nothing
no longer
to suffer

It was nothing
to no longer
suffer, trilling,
this world
is artifice,
your world
is artifice,
it is difficult
to read pain,
its crude wafting,
old wrack

Crude ruin,
old rain
wafting and
just now allegro,
the effulgence
passing, ourselves
and clearest rose,
today is
the excellence,
full sea

A lasting excellence,
full, a total glitter,
sing this of gold will,
a savage house, wind
and its lashes, it is spectacle
pouring down fire,
things the air has de-
composed escape
ululation

Ululating forms
escape composure,
over oceans
wings caw,
generations
to follow, caw,
humanity's
bleak headdress,
an idea

An idea, to love
the bleak headdress
like birds and old
shores ruling,
its companion
cloud, a meta
physical air
transfigured and
clearing, not blue

A blue metaphysical
clearing air, translates
a doppler whine
in the unicameral mind,
a taper solos, billows,
a cheering sun bedazzles

Bedazzled and
blossoming,
a taper flame
in cheering sun,
day's piping
opens up
the greenest
among us,
knows the wind,
its quest
phase shifting,
sotto voce

*iii.*

Phase shifting,
sotto voce,
now wind,
its question,
a celestial ditty,
subvocalized
in the awesome
ontic day, in
ordinary chroma,
in lucent arias,
the greenest ones

Between flashy arias
the day calls to
the present animal
incarnate presence,
the blush, breath,
tinct and undertone,
the gusto, horrid
kingdom of ens

This gusting
kingdom
has no end
but hoary
when the brain
is slow
to compose
the word,
when the word
is too large
but cannot
contain it,
hear ghost,
sing air

The ghosting
florals alive
and singing,
to pass by
molecules
and floaters,
see past
the little
creatures
in your eye,
wind speeds,
some thing

These things
in the eye,
sozzled praise,
sweet, when
the mind
is right size,
taking the sky,
its milky band
at midnight,
the chimes faint,
the day's hypo
dissolving into
a gogic slur

Stinging chimes
evolve into a
hypno-blur, bees
attending the bell,
regular sounds
of circadia buzz
then bang, some lead
in the chest, covered
in rags and money
this flat fore-
shortened world

Like a world
foreshortened, flat,
big petals flying,
big petals re-
wiring the word
in absolute
lucent ash,
the absolute
of a mind,
a lucent mind
in weather,
in the auroral
phenom's tinct

Lost in weather, in
the phenom's auroral ting,
a sapphire core becomes
a mystic choir and
the blue fat dawn
in morning's scatter,
a musical ground,
speckled glass reflecting

A musical ground,
the speckled glass
reflecting the fine-string
half-tones of ens,
fabled architectures,
the cables braiding
marigolds
in string light, in
air and incense

Light is a string
built of motes
in ayres and incense,
a marigold tonality,
cabled and wither-
ward fabled, parti-
colored, this magick
eye plays tricks in
morning's coloratura

# 3. NOCTURNE

# SHIP OF STATE

1.

I wandered all night with my corpse... passed over the scene... saw the rubble and war debris... I felt it... it was human... I sat next to the corpse... I kept vigil everywhere... it traveled with me... down streets... on walks... in coffee shops... it became indistinguishable from my own form... from my own... I often wonder if people see it... see me... consider the corpse in front of the night sky... it was the particulate vocal pattern that is mine... was in fact mine...

2.

when the voice says this is your room now… it has been arranged for you… the room alive speaks when the corpse speaks… and the earth speaks this estate of dirt… this is your room… it has been arranged for you… this room with its satin and its sash… with its velvet and its black… its paper and glue… some pages sewn… a room so plush so deep saying… this is your room now… take care…

3.

the corpse was joy... the joy was forever... transitive and ever... everything going off at various intervals all at once humming and ill harmonizing... the larger ongoing... the cold matter... dark... and the trans of that nimbus... of that... of which... no longer of... sing... the organs gel... become waxy... slowly congeal... a thickening quickens throughout... at first patchy... then a wooden feeling... changing states and stranger codes... I was here and not here I was everywhere and slid easily out of the head and had no shape... had no... whoa... whoa... the cyclone kept faster and then all... ticking... hammering... ringing... slight tings... a distant volume increasing and... every inanimate thing emitting a stronger sound... a note... a click... popping popping... a total bell ringer... I was now and not now... a something in a world of things... a piece of petrified dizzy... the stars were screaming brass... I could hear their gain... a symphony of the gone... a heady vertigo... an orchestral whatchamacallit... and the dead welcomed me as they... now we... listened to the banging... I was tuning... a wood chime thinging when the putrefied lips of the corpses curled a bit to smile at me...

4.

to enter a paper-like glen… gullies speckled with moon and moss… and those surface effects on water… music too gently pulsed at first… then broke into swoon… and now I remain each line opened… before summer deepened like tone on flesh… and how does a boy begin to love a corpse… a stinking mass of rotten flesh…

5.

I wrote to speak to my autopsy... my dropsy... my falling sickness... I wrote one season forever changing into the night sky... I wrote to see the core as my corpse... began to open up to that surround...

6.

some people survive battle… some their childhood… some survive nothing… some children are forever lost in their body… wave upon wave… voices… sound effects… phantasmagoria… there is no return… only the idea… there is no return only narrative… to survive is to…

7.

I wandered all night with my corpse... passed over the scene... I was waking and I was dawning... to watch moonlight cross a face... the features change in shadow... the changing features of a mind... when I spoke to the corpse it was as though I spoke to the curtains or the rug... the body lay there in permanent discourse with the object world... the curtain... the rug... the candle... the ring... now on speaking terms with the corpse... and they were singing to each other... I was happy to be free with my corpse... this was the total... the ongoing... I was deranged and deregulated... I was free of property... I was earth... and it was myself circling the sun... to be simply here then simply gone... to follow the moon's path... the scatter on water... to become that report... passing over trees and garbage alike... decomposing and flowering... and the life of rot and the body there... immobile... that the trees and grass are speaking to it... for it... the bones... the head... the gone gaze in the eye...

8.

see this town from a hill field standing... a scenic postcard lit from yesteryear... or the soft lines of a small town seen from a distance... a local boneyard sleeping time away... the open landscape we face together... sky changes... momently...

9.

consider the brow... consider the head... its incandescent globe-like quality... that it's loved... consider the brow... consider the head... its globe-like ascendancy... consider the eye... the eye socket... the aperture... the opening of the eye dilated in love or death... consider the years since anyone's offing... since that tree went down this field hasn't felt the same... consider the corpse... the rich life of ions... the unstable reanimation of flesh and grass... consider the prow... its translation... consider the night boat on its way with the soul... consider its passage... historically we think it an easy ride in a small bark from shore to shore... but there are many boats and glutted waters... see the yachts and liners... gondolas... and tugs... many vessels tossed in water... skiffs... canoes... trawlers... junks... all of them full... stalled... discontented and decaying... as it is... so then... as here... so there... it figures... the light is filled with dead people...

# 4. CODA

## FROM THIS END OF SADNESS

A particular blur
attended my mind
from end to end.

These feelings
of futurelessness.

To free fall into it.

It feels like winter,
the light overcast
and the day lit up
from within.

To find a line in it.

I found a world
torched into renewal,

blackened stalks
pointing skyward.

I took fortification
from goneness.
At this end
the notation is green.

No stopping music
entering air
and tearing air,
the songs
were old songs.

They came
with the wren
and the robin.
Also the crow
so dear to reality
and elegy
and traffic,
its essential din.

The synesthesia
of the din.

From this end
of sadness
I identified
the voice as dead,
it was companionable.
I identified sky
turning topaz.

I did not
understand shadows,
did not understand
luminosity.

I did not understand
the code that held
me to the world.

From this end
glistening leaves,
cool air.

Wandering out into it,
wondering through it,
the day crumbles to dust
inside a blue dahlia.

I am that dust and dahlia.

I am coeval
with the rotting trunk
and the pine needles
regenerating soil.

I am happiest
with the forest floor,
branches listing
under a porcelain sky.

I'm into that medieval
light glancing
through leaves.
The tree's arches
are a great
kingdom now.

From this end
of sadness
there's nothing
out there I want
and wonder
if there's anything
in here I need?

I'm into the way
the technology of an I
is filled with the dead.

I'm heavy with light
when the old sun
is speaking,
when I'm not sure
the day is real.

When it's hard
to be in and of it,
to be here with it
and under it.

From this end of sadness
shapes come,
all the boldest shadows.

From this end animals,
the oldest eyes,
the *cri de coeur*,
afternoons hung
with seeping light.

Poor sun,
waiting to die.
Poor sun
solo in space,
fueling
our heads,
a tiny sun
in the mind.

Right now,
a particle
decays
on the lawn.

From this end
gravity decays
in the mind.

To never forget
the corners
and dust bunnies
of the laughing sun.

But if the song
weren't a bright star
hanging in
the firmament
then what
can be said
for burning embers
in the fire.

I see you turning
and bending there
in the cold dream
of the past
braiding

with the now
of blur.

Blur with me
when I am sick
of dying,
fearful of failing
the song I love.

Be with me
whenever I sit
wasting days.

Comfort the hours.

# ACKNOWLEDGMENTS

Thanks to the many editors of journals and anthologies where these poems appeared: *Boston Review*, *The Brooklyn Rail*, *The Cambridge Literary Review* (UK), *The Caught Habits of Language* (UK), *The Chicago Review*, *Conjunctions*, *Erizo* (Mexico), *The Forward Book of Poetry* (UK), *Granta* (UK), *Hambone*, *Harper's*, *Hyperallergic*, *Jubilat*, *Mississippi Review*, *Mote* (UK), *New York Review of Books*, *Paris Review*, *The Poetry Review* (UK), *Splinter* (UK), *The Stinging Fly* (Ireland), *Vallum* (Canada), and *The World Speaking Back* (UK).

Poems have also appeared in limited-edition volumes; many thanks to Jon Beacham for *New Poems*, The Brother in Elysium: Kingston, New York; David Grundy for *Marigold & Cable*, Materials: Cambridge, UK; and Guy Pettit for *The Afterlife of Paper* (with collages by Richard Kraft), Catalpa: Los Angeles, California.

The series "Marigold & Cable" was commissioned by the composer Alex Cobb to accompany his LP of the same title.

The poem "Letter to the Ghost World" was a limited broadside, printed letterpress with an original film still by Jon Beacham, The Brother in Elysium: Kingston, New York.

The poem "Ship of State," was handset and printed as an artist book in an edition of twelve with original collages by Jon Beacham, The Brother in Elysium: Kingston, New York.

Thanks to the good folks at MacDowell Colony and the University of Cambridge for time and focus.

And last but not least, my deepest thanks to my brilliant friends who read poems and drafts, made astute comments, and supported me during the writing of this book.

# INDEX OF TITLES

Archival Light  *47*
Every Day I Want to Fly My Kite  *11*
From this End of Sadness  *101*
Inside Out Loud  *34*
Last Poem  *26*
Letter to the Ghost World  *40*
Marigold & Cable  *57*
Now It's Dark *(No one gave me a greater thing)*  *30*
Now It's Dark *(Not the easiest day I'm having)*  *18*
Out of the World in Real Time  *24*
Ship of State  *89*
Sky Burial  *32*
Some Joy for Morning  *50*
Speech Acts for a Dying World  *3*
Sunday's Empire  *46*
Sunshine  *51*
That I Saw the Light on Nonotuck Avenue  *8*
The Afterlife of Paper  *23*
The Blossom Is Stronger than Us  *54*
The Face Is a Political Animal  *44*
The Ingenuity of Animal Survival  *43*
The Present Is Constant Elegy  *16*
Vastation  *41*

# ABOUT THE AUTHOR

PETER GIZZI is the author of eight collections of poetry, most recently, *Archeophonics* (Finalist for the 2016 National Book Award), *In Defense of Nothing*, and *Threshold Songs*. His honors include the Lavan Younger Poet Award from the Academy of American Poets, and fellowships in poetry from The Rex Foundation, The Fund for Poetry, The Howard Foundation, The Foundation for Contemporary Arts, and The John Simon Guggenheim Memorial Foundation. He has twice been the recipient of The Judith E. Wilson Visiting Fellowship in Poetry at the University of Cambridge. His editing projects have included *o·blēk: a journal of language arts*, *The Exact Change Yearbook*, *The House That Jack Built: The Collected Lectures of Jack Spicer*, and, with Kevin Killian, *My Vocabulary Did This to Me: The Collected Poetry of Jack Spicer*. He works at the University of Massachusetts, Amherst.

LIBRARY OF CONGRESS CATALOGING-IN-PUBLICATION DATA
Names: Gizzi, Peter, author.
Title: Now it's dark / Peter Gizzi.
Description: Middletown, Connecticut : Wesleyan University Press, [2020] |
   Series: Wesleyan poetry | Includes index.
Identifiers: LCCN 2020004231 (print) | LCCN 2020004232 (ebook) |
   ISBN 9780819579867 (cloth) | ISBN 9780819579874 (trade paperback) |
   ISBN 9780819579881 (ebook)
Subjects: LCGFT: Poetry.
Classification: LCC PS3557.I94 N69 2020 (print) | LCC PS3557.I94 (ebook) |
   DDC 811/.54—dc23
LC record available at https://lccn.loc.gov/2020004231
LC ebook record available at https://lccn.loc.gov/2020004232